a morning cup of
prayer
for mothers

CRANE HILL
PUBLISHERS

Published by Crane Hill Publishers
www.cranehill.com

Book design by Miles G. Parsons
Illustrations by Tim Rocks and Christena Brooks
Cover art by Christena Brooks

Printed in China

Library of Congress Cataloging-in-Publication Data

Bright-Fey, J. (John)
    A morning cup of prayer for mothers / John Bright-Fey. -- Crane Hill ed.
        p. cm.
    ISBN-13: 978-1-57587-264-3
    ISBN-10: 1-57587-264-1
    1. Mothers--Religious life. 2. Prayer--Christianity. 3. Prayers. I. Title.
    BV4529.18.B74 2006
    248.3'20852--dc22

                                                    2006016161

a morning cup of prayer
for mothers

A daily guided devotional for a lifetime
of inspiration and peace

john a. bright-fey

CRANE HILL
PUBLISHERS

Acknowledgments

I would like to thank the following individuals for their invaluable help and advice. This Morning Cup would surely not taste as sweet without their assistance:

To Professor Tom Gibbs for talking me into teaching college classes on prayer and contemplative living;
To all of my students whose experience of prayer and faith has profoundly moved me and deeply informed my work;
To Ellen, Linda, and all the staff and artists at Crane Hill Publishers for giving me this glorious opportunity;
To my amazing wife, Kim, who helps me in more ways than she could possibly know;
To the many men and women of faith that have, through the years, guided and shaped my life of prayer.

I thank God for each of you.

Dedication

In Loving Memory
Viola Gertrude Patricia Caverlee Marshall
"Grandma Vi"

Thanks for teaching me how to listen.

Contents

I tell you the truth, my Father will give you whatever you ask in my name. Until now you have not asked for anything in my name. Ask and you will receive, and your joy will be complete.
—John 16:23-24

Foreword

Are you a mother or mother-to-be than wants closer contact with God? If your answer is "Yes," then this book was written for you. With it you can begin an incredible journey for yourself or a loved one into the heart of God. Both the means to begin this journey and the power to sustain it for a lifetime are the same: prayer.

Part devotional and part instruction manual, this *Morning Cup of Prayer* is designed to be a spiritual patchwork quilt of advice, wisdom and inspiration for those who have answered His call to motherhood. With it you will learn how to actively take Him with you throughout your day and be continuously nourished by His Grace.

I've tried to write this book so that you would be able to absorb its contents as easily as possible. I say that "I wrote" this book, but in truth my hand was guided by God and it's contents formed by His Grace. I felt His love with every word. Now, it is my sincerest wish that you feel it as well, and, for the sake of all His children, come to know Him as never before.

Mothers and Prayer

I don't think it's an overstatement to say that mothers have the most important job in the world. In light of that, it astounds me that there are so many mothers who do not pray.

To be sure, as a man, I am on the outside looking in. But it seems to me that women who have picked up the mantle of "Motherhood" deserve all of the help and support we can give them. No matter how hard we as men try to help, their greatest source of aid and comfort comes from the helping hand of our Heavenly Father. And He is reached through prayer.

The problems that face mothers yield readily to prayer's power. Prayer can change the course of an individual life or the life of a nation. Families torn apart by strife, disaster, or indifference can be made whole again with prayer. It can cure the worst physical illnesses and heal the deepest emotional wounds. If we become lost, it helps us to find our way again.

Prayer knows. It pulls us back from the brink of what is toxic and shows us where and when to move forward towards personal nourishment and the nourishment of our families. Most importantly, prayer is our birthright as God's children. It energizes, strengthens, comforts, informs, supports, and protects us. Simply put, prayer reclaims lives, futures, and souls. It is easily the most important tool a mother can possess.

With all that prayer has to offer, why then don't more mothers pray? The answer is simple: they don't know how.

Perhaps you are a mother who needs the complete wholeness that prayer provides but are confused about the subject. Maybe you don't think that you have the time to pray properly. Any number of everyday events can leave you feeling as though you just don't know how, when, or where to pray. The book you are now holding will solve those problems. It will help you find the time and energy to pray without sacrificing the needs of your family. It will help you clear a path between you and your greatest strength and show you the way to prayer.

I've divided this book into roughly three parts. The first will be a discussion of the special needs of mothers that can be addressed by prayer. I have always felt that God favors women in matters of prayer. His Word also reveals a special covenant with women who become mothers. Our Savior Jesus Christ was a strong advocate of both women and motherhood. Our Heavenly Father provides mothers His protection and the promise of safety. He wants you to infuse your family with His Word and His Grace.

Yet, so many mothers have become mired in the conflicts and complexities of modern life. They become assailed by demands that were unknown to their own mothers. Running a household, raising children and, in more and more cases, holding down a job can be overwhelming. How is it possible to honor God's Will in all of it? The key to becoming the kind of mother God wants you to become is prayer.

The second part of this book will be a discussion of the mechanics of prayer and some of its methods. I will also discuss what a prayerful life can look like.

Most often, when someone tells me, "I don't pray," what they are really saying is, "I don't know what to say to God." If you are one of those individuals, please don't worry. In the third part of this book, I will present you with an assortment of Biblically based prayers and relevant passages from His Word that both support and augment them.

Each scriptural prayer was especially written with the needs of mothers in mind. They are grouped with the scripture passages that, I think, most mothers will find suitable for contemplation and prayer. Take your time when perusing them as there is much wisdom they bring to the table.

Please look upon these prayers as suggestions. True prayer is a profoundly personal thing that must come from your heart. Think of the prayers and passages in this book as starting points for your personal spiritual journey. Use them to get comfortable with the act of praying. Then, as guided by the Holy Spirit, you will learn to speak the language of prayer.

In the time it would take for you to have a pleasant cup of tea before the children wake up in the morning—or even after you've put them to bed at night—you can begin your spiritual journey and sustain it for a lifetime.

I think it's important for all mothers to remember something that, ultimately, they will understand better than anyone else. Your prayers don't mold, define, and nourish your own family, exclusively. Because of your special place as mothers, you are influencing the spiritual lives of future generations. It's a big job, but I know you're up to the task. Before you begin, would you like to share a Morning Cup with me?

JBF
Birmingham, Alabama
2006

Ask, and it will be given to you; seek and you will find;
knock and the door will be opened to you. For everyone
who asks receives; he who seeks finds; and to him who
knocks, the door will be opened.
—Matthew 7:7-8

Why Mothers Need Prayer

Recently, I asked a group of women to share their thoughts on prayer and motherhood. Specifically, I wanted to know what situations and circumstances would, should, and have sent them to their knees in prayer. The list they produced revealed many of the wonders, the blessings, and the trials of being a mother. Here are the highlights:

- Learning that you are going to be a mother
- Resolving the conflict between gladness and fear during pregnancy
- Feeling endlessly fatigued
- Choosing between career and family
- Balancing the demands of career and family
- Maintaining a marriage while being a homemaker

- Being a single mother
- Guilt
- Uninvolved, abusive, or indifferent husband
- Divorce
- Loss of individuality
- Loss of a child
- Loss of a husband
- Boredom with the routine
- Pride
- Finding joy
- Safety
- Dealing with the abuse of a family member
- Being a compassionate and caring mother
- Declaration of war
- World catastrophe and the suffering it produces
- Feeling isolated
- Feeling abandoned by those you love
- Managing a relationship with your own mother
- Learning that your child is going to be a parent

These are all valid issues, to be sure. But the most amazing and informative reason for prayer, to me at least, was giving up motherhood. In essence, each of my panel felt that prayer would help them find the strength and wisdom to work themselves out of the world's most satisfying and challenging job: being a mother.

The Noble Wife

I remember the first time I read the thirty-first chapter of Proverbs. It knocked me out. In verses 10-31 was the description of the perfect wife and mother.

A wife of noble character who can find?
She is worth far more than rubies.

Her husband has full confidence in her
and lacks nothing of value.

She brings him good, not harm,
all the days of her life.

She selects wool and flax
and works with eager hands.

She is like the merchant ships,
bringing her food from afar.

She gets up while it is still dark;
she provides food for her family
and portions for her servant girls.

She considers a field and buys it;
out of her earnings she plants a vineyard.

She sets about her work vigorously;
her arms are strong for her tasks.

She sees that her trading is profitable,
and her lamp does not go out at night.

In her hand she holds the distaff
and grasps the spindle with her fingers.

She opens her arms to the poor
and extends her hands to the needy.

When it snows, she has no fear for her household;
for all of them are clothed in scarlet.

She makes coverings for her bed;
she is clothed in fine linen and purple.

Her husband is respected at the city gate,
where he takes his seat among the elders of the land.

She makes linen garments and sells them,
and supplies the merchants with sashes.

She is clothed with strength and dignity;
she can laugh at the days to come.

She speaks with wisdom,
and faithful instruction is on her tongue.

She watches over the affairs of her household
and does not eat the bread of idleness.

Her children arise and call her blessed;
her husband also, and he praises her:

"Many women do noble things,
but you surpass them all."

Charm is deceptive, and beauty is fleeting;
but a woman who fears the LORD is to be praised.

Give her the reward she has earned,
and let her works bring her praise at the city gate.

It strikes me that the qualities expressed in this Proverb are those positive qualities inherent not only in wives and mothers, but in all women. The real challenge for mothers is allowing those inherent qualities to come forth and manifest fully. This requires the courage to honestly confront yourself in the face of your own uncertainty. When meeting the responsibility of caring for children, there is little margin for error.

I believe that, when guided by the Holy Spirit, each of us knows full well the extent of our gifts and our deficits. We intrinsically know what to do to conquer our fears and address those issues that stand between us and our being the person God knows us to be. We have but to do it. They key to accessing the wisdom and strength necessary to solve those problems is prayer.

If you would like to be the kind of mother God knows you to be then it's time to take the key of prayer and through Christ Jesus enter your Father's house to seek His wisdom. If you can imagine the smiles of your children, then you can pray from your heart. If you can pray from your heart, then you will be shown how to overcome any of the problems you face. It's as simple as that.

What Is Prayer?

The stated goal of this book is to teach mothers how to pray. In order to do that, we need a definition of precisely what "praying" is. We also need to discuss the different kinds of prayer and the best ways to approach them. Before we get much further, though, I have a story about an amazing wife and mother that might help us get things off to a good start and insure a great finish.

A Mother's Example of Prayer

My inspiration for this book on prayer and the model I use for conducting a prayerful life come from someone very dear to me.

Everything I know about prayer I learned from my maternal grandmother, Viola. Grandma Vi was a devout churchgoer and easily the most amazing Christian that you'd ever be likely to meet. To be fair, I've learned a lot about prayer, contemplation, and devotion from many other wonderful men and women of faith. But the lessons from Grandma remain to this day the most profound, direct, and the most useful that I've ever received. Everything she did—whether it was homemaking, teaching music, comforting a friend or being a wife and grandmother—she approached with prayer.

Every morning after putting away the breakfast dishes, Grandma Vi would quietly announce that she was going to her room to "talk with God." She would then retire to the back bedroom, close the door, and do precisely that. Forty-five minutes to an hour later, she would emerge renewed, refreshed—transformed really—confident, self assured, and positively radiant.

No matter what difficulties life presented her, the negative would literally fade away as her smile and countenance pushed back the gloom. The grace she radiated was as palpable and real as gravity. You could feel it; you could almost hold it in your hand. No matter what kind of ugly mood had you by the scruff of the neck, her smile set you free. Grandma had just finished talking with God and everything was, profoundly, right with the world.

Talking with God

I cannot remember how young I was when I first realized that Grandma said, "talk with God" instead of the usual "talk to God" that most people say when discussing prayer. Indeed, the transformation that would occur within her bespoke of something much more than simply a one-sided long distance conversation. I mean, it looked like she and God had actually been sitting in her room having a chat!

When I asked her what she and God talked about, she would reply, "Oh, all kinds of things." "Big stuff?" I asked. "Yes," she said "but, small things, too. I ask Him to watch over you and the rest of the family. If I have a problem I ask for His help and the strength to take care of it the way that He wants me to. I thank Him for all of the happiness and blessing He has given me. Most of the time, though, God talks and I listen to Him. You have to listen if you're going to have a real conversation with God. He likes it when we listen, just the way I like it when you listen to me. After all, He loves me the way that I love you."

"Do you only talk to God in your room?" I asked. "No," she said. "He meets me here." As she spoke she touched my heart with her hand. "I talk with Him here." That made me feel good and I remember thinking in a child's way that while it was important to love God, it was far more important to let Him love you.

Trust in the Lord with all your heart and lean not on your own understanding; in all your ways acknowledge him, and he will make your paths straight.
—Proverbs 3:5-6

Any Time, Any Place, Any Thing, Any Subject

As I grew older, my fascination with prayer grew, as did my love for God. Yes, our relationship had its rocky moments, but pop culture and arrogant churchmen aside, I never lost contact with Him or forgot how important it was to surrender to His Grace.

Grandma Vi continued to amaze me with her gifts of prayer. When I would drive the twelve hours from college to my grandparents' trailer in Bossier City, Louisiana, she would, quite literally, pray me in. Think about it; she would go about her daily chores with half of her attention actively engaged in a twelve-hour-long continuous prayer for my safe journey. Frequently, she'd have a "message from God" for me when I arrived at the trailer, along with a warm embrace and a home cooked meal that was fit for, well, Jehovah.

Later, when I was rested and ready to drive the additional three hours to home, she would smile and say, "Be careful and be sure to call me when you get to your Mom's house so I know when to quit praying." No matter what time it was, she wouldn't go to sleep until she'd received my call.

I have no doubt that even after I called the trailer to let her know of my safe arrival, she continued to pray. It was clear to me that her whole life was a prayer. That was what I wanted for myself and, over the years, it became what I wanted for everyone else.

Grandma made it plain; a person could—and should—have a heartfelt conversation with God anytime, anywhere, under any circumstances, and about anything.

Different Kinds of Prayer

Grandma's prayers on my behalf were an example of Intercessory prayer, where one person prays for another. There are other kinds of prayer as well.

There are prayers of Thanksgiving and of Praise where we thank our Heavenly Father for the blessings He has given us and give honor to His Grace and Perfect Will. We can obtain more of God through Seeking prayer wherein we simply announce our intention to rest in His presence and allow Him to speak through His Word. Prayers of Confession allow you to repent your sins and ask your Father for the blessing of His forgiveness. Prayers of Supplication involve asking God for His Divine intervention. Submissive prayer or prayers of Surrender involve completely opening up to God's love and welcoming His Grace and Will into our lives.

Different Ways to Pray

Just as there are different kinds of prayer, there are also different ways to pray. You may talk with God silently or aloud. You may mindfully and deliberately repeat passages from the Bible while pondering the meaning of His Word. This is called Repetitive prayer. Prayer can be performed Reflectively by sitting still and coming to know God through the peace of silence or by reflecting on the deeper meaning of His hand at work in your life.

The Most Important Thing about Prayer

Don't let the different kinds of prayer or the different ways to pray confuse you. Remember Grandma Vi's model:

You talk with God (that means listening as well as talking)

- Anytime,
- Anywhere,
- (under) Any circumstances,
- (about) Anything.
- ?

But something is missing. What's vitally important is that your prayers be authentic, that is, they must come from your heart and be in your own voice. Even if you are reading a Biblically based prayer composed by someone else, you must make it real for you. You must see it, feel it, taste it and touch it with everything you've got. So now we have our final "A": Authentically.

You Talk With God

- Anytime
- Anywhere
- Any Circumstances
- Anything
- Authentically

*Therefore I tell you, whatever you ask for in prayer,
believe that you will receive it, and it will be yours.
And when you stand praying, if you hold anything
against anyone, forgive him, so that your Father in
heaven may forgive your sins.*
—Mark 11:24-25

*Sacrifice thank offerings to God, fulfill your vows to
the Most High, and call upon me in the day of
trouble; I will deliver you, and you will honor me.*
—Psalm 50:14-15

Why Should Mothers Pray?

There are so many good reasons for mothers to pray. To start with, reread the list on page 17-18. All of those problems and circumstances can be addressed and solved with prayer. But there are other reasons as well. You can pray:

- for spiritual growth
- for material needs
- for protection from evil
- to confess your sins and ask for forgiveness
- for the sins of others
- for the needs of others
- for the church and its missions
- for others to receive His Word

- for personal healing
- for others to be healed
- for wisdom about any subject
- to help simplify your life
- for personal direction
- to participate in His Holy work around the world

The list could go on forever. When it comes to prayer, you are only as limited as your imagination.

I tell you the truth, my Father will give you whatever you ask in my name. Until now you have not asked for anything in my name. Ask and you will receive, and your joy will be complete.
—John 16:23-24

Prayer is a wonderful gift from our Heavenly Father. He places great value on it and we should avail ourselves of it. So much can be accomplished through the power of prayer. You have but to read the stories of Moses, Samson, Elijah, and the apostle Peter in the Bible to grasp its potential.*

Yet, so often, we feel like we don't have the time or the energy for prayer. Many of us lead such busy lives. Our minds and our bodies work overtime to accomplish the many things we must in order to fulfill our earthly obligations. But when we stop to pray, even if only for a few moments, our whole being changes. We slow our frantic pace, focus on God, and say, "Lord, I love you with all my heart and soul."

Whenever anyone asks me why they should pray, rather than listing the reasons, I say this: "Your Heavenly Father loves you dearly and wants you to visit with Him often. He wants you to come to Him for rest, advice, encouragement, and all manner of council. You can visit anytime you want, day or night. Calling ahead isn't necessary because He is always home waiting for you, His beloved child. There amid the beats of His heart, you will surely find nourishment, comfort, and joy. You will find meaning and direction. If you come to Him when you are sick, He will heal you. No matter how many people are cruel to you or how much life has beaten you down, you can always go to your Father's home. You can tell Him anything and He will be there for you. All you have to do is show up. The doorway to His heart is His son Jesus the Christ and the key to that doorway is prayer." Now that sounds like reason enough for me. How about you?

*Moses (Exodus 15:24-26); Samson (Judges 16:28-30); Elijah (James 5:17,18); Peter (Acts 9:36-41).

For the eyes of the Lord are on the righteous and his ears are attentive to their prayer...
—1 Peter 15:8

The lord detests the sacrifice of the wicked but the prayer of the upright pleases him.
—Proverbs 15:8

Prayer: A Mother's Guide

But when you pray, go into your room, close the door and pray to your Father, who is unseen. Then your Father, who sees what is done in secret, will reward you.
—Matthew 6:6

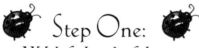

Step One:
Set The Stage With Solitude, Silence, and Stillness

Do you remember how Grandma Vi would go into her room to pray? She was following the instructions laid out in Matthew 6:6. It's the very first thing you should do before you pray: find a place of solitude and enter it.

Your place of solitude can be a room or the corner of a room. It can be your back porch. In truth, it doesn't even have to be a physical structure. Your place of solitude can be out of doors in the deep woods or a even a public park filled with people. It can be any place where you can engineer a feeling of being alone.

When you enter into solitude you enter into the realm of the soul. Here, God gives you the opportunity to drop all pretense and simply be yourself. When you are in solitude you are never really alone. You and your Heavenly Father are there together. That is His promise.

After entering into the realm of the soul, you should then embrace silence and stillness. Here's how you do it.

Generally relax, accept the guidance of the Holy Spirit and tell yourself that you are preparing for prayer, preparing to talk with God. Close your eyes and briefly watch your body and how it naturally moves. For example, your chest rises and falls as you breathe. That's okay; just let it. Perhaps you notice some tension in your neck so you gently drop your shoulders downward a bit to release it. If you notice any physical movement at all, just take notice of it and say to yourself that you'd like to sit as still as you are comfortably able.

Turn your attention to your mind. Other than focusing on God and your intention to pray, don't try to control it in any way. Try not to chastise yourself for a wandering mind that jumps around in the background from one mental topic to the next. Simply acknowledge that your mind is doing something, casually watch it unfold, and keep your focus on your Father and His presence.

You may find it helpful to have soothing music accompany your preparations for prayer. If so, you will enjoy the Morning Cup Audio CD that accompanies this volume. It was designed especially to set the tone for your prayer time.

Settling into a time of prayer is like watching a river flow by out of the corner of your eye. You'll notice obvious things like sailboats, motor craft, tree limbs floating on the surface, even the occasional duck. There are birds flying above the river and fish you cannot see swimming beneath its surface. You're sitting in one place with God but all of the life that is the river flows past you. Enjoy yourself.

After all, you are preparing to talk with God. What could be better than that?

Put a light smile on your face as you allow the river of your mind float to by and you'll begin to notice something: your mind will settle down, your body will relax, and you will begin to feel quiet all over. Sometimes it feels as if you are sensing all of your parts all at once. The best word I know of to describe your sensation is "quiescence." Every part of you settles down and you will feel organized and peaceful. You become bathed in God's Grace and Presence. Now you are ready. This is the canvas upon which you will present your prayers.

It Only Takes a Moment

Though you could spend a lot of time completing your preparations for prayer, it really only takes a moment to engineer solitude, silence, and stillness. With practice you'll be able to set the stage for prayer in an instant.

There is benefit in setting the stage and resting in the realm of the soul for longer periods of time. In this way you utilize solitude, silence, and stillness to reflect and listen for God's wisdom and guidance. There in His loving embrace, you will experience genuine tranquility and perfect peace of mind.

Step Two:
Embrace a Prayerful Attitude

Prayer is so very much more than mere words. It is an attitude that reflects our most heartfelt wishes and hopes. In reality, it's all about heart—your heart to God's heart.

We are all God's children. As a parent He isn't gruff or unfeeling, yet we often approach Him as if He is. Our Father is love itself and the secret to true prayer is simple: we must be His children.

I often ask people who pray regularly to listen to themselves as they pray. "Try it for yourself," I say. "How do you sound when you pray? Do you sound like an outsider intruding upon God's quiet repose? Do you plead or beg? Do your words impose or do you sound like a child talking with a beloved parent?"

That last example, of course, is how it should be. We should not sound like spiritual panhandlers. We are God's loving and obedient children and behaving in that way is the secret key to true and authentic prayer.

Every Mother Is Unique

In His wisdom, our Heavenly Father created each of us to be a unique individual. When He gave us the gift of prayer He knew that each of us would have our own unique way of speaking with Him. That's precisely the way He wants it. He wants each of us to be completely honest and authentic by expressing what's in our heart to Him. Remember, whether you offer spontaneous prayers or prayers composed by someone else, you must feel it in your heart.

Step Three:
Choose Your Method of Prayer

There are many ways that mothers can pray. For this Morning Cup I've chosen four ways that you may engage in prayer:

Spoken Prayer

Simply put, speak aloud. Declaiming your prayers out loud has a special quality to it. When you taste what you are saying, the words have a greater effect upon you and your prayers become powerful.

Silent Prayer

Silent prayers are more intimate than spoken ones. Praying in this way brings a delicate and private quality to your worship. Use silent prayer whenever you feel the need to more personally connect with your Heavenly Father.

Repetitive Prayer

Repeat your prayer over and over. You may do this aloud or silently in your mind. However, no matter how you choose to say the prayer, it is important that each repetition be mindful and deliberate. Mindlessly repeating words is not praying. Repetitive, authentic prayer produces a profoundly focused communication with God.

Reflective Prayer

Reflective prayer is performed in silence. Simply read a Biblical passage or any prayer that you choose and silently reflect on its meaning. Just hold the thought of the prayer in your heart and mind. The Holy Spirit does the rest. Reflective prayer engenders peaceful communication with God and reveals His Wisdom.

Step Four:
Talk with God

All of the prayers that make up the balance of this book have been composed, and the Bible selections chosen, with the idea of using them in any one of the above prayer methods outlined in Step Three. Of course, you can dispense with them altogether and speak with your Father according to the dictates of your heart. But what if you have never prayed before?

Do you remember my comments in the beginning about mothers who say that they don't know how to pray? All too often, they really just don't know what to say to God. If you are one of those people then you probably remember that I also told you not to worry.

The next section of this book contains all the suggestions you need to learn how to speak the language of prayer. Please learn from it and let it inspire you to lead a prayerful life. Your Father is in His home and He would dearly love to speak with you.

Step Five:
Listen to God

The fifth and final step of prayer is probably the most important. At least it was for Grandma Vi. Do you remember what she said about how she spent most of her prayer time? That's right; she spent it listening.

Please remember, authentic prayer is a conversation filled with devotion and love that takes place between you and your Heavenly Father. Prayer is so incredibly precious to God. It releases an enormous outpouring of His wisdom, power, inspiration and strength. But you have to listen and you have to listen patiently.

After speaking to Him, ask God to speak back to you in any way He sees fit. You may use the journal that begins on page 71 to record any important thoughts and insights that come up, especially when He speaks to you through His Word. Let Him call your attention to those areas in your life where He wants to help.

Spend as much time listening to God as you would like. One minute of really listening to God would be great. Fifteen would be so much better. You choose. An hour listening to God isn't too much, and neither is a lifetime.

Let us then labor for an inward stillness,
An inward stillness and an inward healing;
That perfect silence where lips and heart
Are still, and we no longer entertain
Our own imperfect thoughts and vain opinions,
But God alone speaks in us, and we wait
In singleness of heart, that we may know
God's will, and in the silence of our spirit,
That we may do God's will and do that only.
—Longfellow, The Christus

A Mother's Life  Inspired By Prayer

I've always loved the word "inspired." It means, "in-spirit." When my publisher approached me to write several books on prayer for the Morning Cup series she could hardly have known that on those mornings after my grandmother had chatted with God, she would, invariably, make a cup of tea, sit down, leisurely sip, and bask in the glow of being "in spirit." I can think of no better way to start a day or spend a life. Can you?

The Lord's Prayer

This, then, is how you should pray:
"Our Father in heaven,
hallowed be your name,

your kingdom come,
your will be done
on earth as it is in heaven.

Give us today our daily bread.
Forgive us our debts,
as we also have forgiven our debtors.

And lead us not into temptation,
but deliver us from the evil one."
—*Matthew* 6:9-13

Prayers for Mothers

Whenever your life as a mother makes you feel tense, nervous, and uncertain, it is time to surrender through prayer. Authentic prayer is a fundamental rededication of your faith every time you engage in it. It brings the peace of the Father to you by helping you to completely open up to His love, wisdom, strength, and forgiveness.

Relax your heart and bring peace to your soul by surrendering all of your cares and worries to God through prayer. What doubts could you possibly have when you are resting in your Father's loving arms while being filled with His Grace?

Prayers

As you begin to incorporate prayer into your life, you may find it helpful to have examples of prayers to get you started. Here are some samples that, along with selected scripture passages, will set the tone for prayer. As you make these initial steps, the Holy Spirit will help you in your efforts.

A Prayer of Surrender

Father, in the name of Jesus, I surrender to the Holy Spirit. I come to You as a mother and ask You to fill my soul with Your Grace and let me lead the life that You have set out for me. Amen.

A Prayer for Wisdom

Father, You have granted unto me the wisdom and guidance I require to do Your bidding. You have hidden this wisdom in the very substance of Your miracle. It is through Your Son, Christ Jesus that this wisdom is available to all. Help me to receive it in His name. Thank You, Father.

A Prayer for Protection

Heavenly Father, for the sake of my family, help me to surrender fully to Your love. Please watch over them the way You watch over me. Amen.

A Prayer of Submission

Lord, at this very moment I submit to You, become Your disciple and follow You. In Jesus' name I pray.

You were taught, with regard to your former way of life, to put off your old self, which is being corrupted by its deceitful desires; to be made new in the attitude of your minds and to put on the new self, created to be like God in true righteousness and holiness.
—Ephesians 4:22-24

A Prayer for Refreshment

Lord, help me to yield to Your Grace and
surrender to Your Perfect Will. I am burdened
and work so very hard, yet, at times I feel that I
will never complete my labors. But in You I
always find welcome rest and repose. I accept
Your peace. Thank You, Father.

A Prayer for Instruction

Heavenly Father, please teach me how to take
care of my family without neglecting myself in
the process. Grant me the strength and wisdom
to be a good mother. I know that through Your
Grace I will never lose touch with who I am
because I will never lose touch with You. In
Jesus' name I pray.

A Prayer for Healing

Father, I come to You in the name of Jesus, out
of concern for the health of my child. Please heal
his body and raise him up. Grant me the wisdom
to tend to his sickness. Let him live a long and
healthy life and spread the good news of Your
Word, for it is by Your Word that You heal us all.
Amen.

*And the prayer offered in faith will make the sick person
well; the Lord will raise him up. If he has sinned, he will
be forgiven.*
—James 5:15

He sent forth his word and healed them;
he rescued them from the grave.
—*Psalm* 107:20

And if the Spirit of him who raised Jesus from the dead
is living in you, he who raised Christ from the dead will
also give life to your mortal bodies through his Spirit,
who lives in you.
—*Romans* 8:11

A Prayer of Peace

Father, in the name Jesus, I ask You to calm my mind and bring order to my thoughts. If I could rest for only a moment in Your loving arms it would help me to cut through the delusions, self-pity, and fears that are afflicting me. Give me Your strength, Lord so that I may conquer this depression and again hear Your plans in my heart. Let my mind be shaped according to Your Perfect Will. Amen.

In righteousness you will be established:
Tyranny will be far from you;
you will have nothing to fear.
Terror will be far removed;
it will not come near you.
—Isaiah 54:14

Your attitude should be the same as that of Christ Jesus:
—*Philippians 2:5*

A Prayer of Guidance

Lord, please keep watch over my children's teachers and guide their hands according to Your Divine Will. Let Your wisdom enter their hearts and protect them. Amen.

For wisdom will enter your heart,
and knowledge will be pleasant to your soul.

Discretion will protect you,
and understanding will guard you.

Wisdom will save you from the ways of wicked men,
from men whose words are perverse,
—Proverbs 2:10-12

A Prayer for Leadership

Dearest Lord, in all things, let me know Your Perfect Will. Guide and lead me as I grow along with my family. Let us all know Your plan. Let us all know Your love. In Jesus' name I pray, Amen.

You have made known to me the path of life;
you will fill me with joy in your presence,
with eternal pleasures at your right hand.
—Psalm 16:11

A Prayer for Purity

Heavenly Father, help me to live a life influenced
and shaped by the Holy Spirit. Help me to turn
away from corruptible things and search for
those things that promote and delight the Spirit.
In the name of Jesus I pray, Amen.

Do not merely listen to the word, and so deceive
yourselves. Do what it says.
—James 1:22

But the wisdom that comes from heaven is first of all pure; then peace-loving, considerate, submissive, full of mercy and good fruit, impartial and sincere.
—James 3:17

A Prayer of Commitment

Dearest Father, I bring my children before you and place them in your loving care. Guide and protect them so they may come to know you in the fullness of your most Holy Spirit. Amen.

The unfolding of your words gives light; it gives understanding to the simple.
—Psalm 119:130

*Nor should there be obscenity, foolish talk or coarse
joking, which are out of place, but rather thanksgiving.*
—*Ephesians 5:4*

A Prayer of Thanks

Father, thank you for Your Word of Life. Please
all children to discover the wonders of Your
Divine wisdom and grant them understanding
and appreciation of Your plan for them. In Jesus'
name I pray, Amen.

An Extra Sip

Prayerwalking

Whenever the demands of a home and family overwhelm you, and you feel the pace of life start to run over you, it's time for walking prayers or Prayerwalking.

Every time you take a step you have the opportunity for prayer. In many ways, walking prayers can have more impact on you than standing, kneeling, or sitting while you pray. This is because your entire body is in motion when you walk just as it is when you are going about your daily tasks. It is instrumental in teaching you how to pray during any activity and, eventually, to pray without ceasing.

Prayerwalking intrinsically reminds us of our connection to God's miracle, that is the earth. When we walk we feel it beneath our feet. We know it with our whole body just as we know about our Heavenly connection to our Father through our souls. Walking prayers enliven your senses, clear your thinking, and can energize you to God's Word. If you ever need reaffirmation of your chosen path in life or if you are having a hard time standing your ground for what you believe in, then pray as you walk.

Walking prayers are best done when you are alone. Anywhere you can walk slowly and deliberately will be suitable for these prayers. I prefer the outdoors, be it a city park, the woods, or your back yard. The choice is yours. It is important to bring a sense of stillness to your walk.

Pretend that the prayers are delicate and that a hurried pace might break them. Be gentle with yourself. As you walk among the many gifts that He has placed for us on this world, know that each step you take brings you closer to Him.

If you choose to walk in a public place, be sure to not to call attention to what you are doing. But take the opportunity to pray for people you see along the way. If you pass someone who is obviously ill, then pray for them. If you see someone giving into sin, pray for their deliverance. You can walk around your home, garden, campus, or city hall and bring the power of prayer with you everywhere. Simply, walk and talk with God.

Walking Prayers

I walk with God in peace and contentment.
I walk with God and recognize His gifts to
me.
I walk with God and am nourished by His
loving kindness.
I walk with God and am healed and
strengthened by His Grace.
I walk with God and extend His love to
everyone.
I walk with God knowing that He is with me
always.
I walk with God and am filled with the Holy
Spirit.
I walk with God and breathe in His mercy.
I walk with God knowing His Perfect Will.
I walk with God upon a bedrock of His Word
and bring the light of His message to the
world.
In Jesus' name I pray, Amen.

A Prayer for Cleansing

Father, in the name of Jesus, let me banish pain, disease and evil with each and every step I take. Amen.

Have mercy on me, O God, according to your unfailing love; according to your great compassion blot out my transgressions. Wash away all my iniquity and cleanse me from my sin.
—Psalm 51: 1-2

But if we walk in the light, as he is in the light, we have fellowship with one another, and the blood of Jesus, his Son, purifies us from all sin.
—1 John 1: 7

A Prayer for Forgiveness

Father, You know that there have been those
who have persecuted me. Help me to love them.
Let each step I take be one of forgiveness.
Through You I know that mine are the steps that
bless the world and everyone in it.

Commit your way to the LORD;
trust in him and he will do this:
—Psalm 37:5

Bless those who persecute you; bless and do not curse.
—Romans 12:14

But I tell you: Love your enemies and pray for those who persecute you.
—*Matthew 5:44*

And hope does not disappoint us, because God has poured out his love into our hearts by the Holy Spirit, whom he has given us.
—*Romans 5:5*

An Affirmation
As I walk, I walk with God and His love.

. . .ask where the good way is, and walk in it, and you
will find rest for your souls.
—Jeremiah 6:16

And this is my prayer: that your love may abound more
and more in knowledge and depth of insight, so that you
may be able to discern what is best and may be pure and
blameless until the day of Christ, filled with the fruit of
righteousness that comes through Jesus Christ—to the
glory and praise of God.
—Philippians 1:9-11

Walking in Love

In Jesus' name, I walk. As I do I extend the love
of God to everyone I meet. My steps are Yours.
With them I banish fear and bring Your Grace.

*But if anyone obeys his word, God's love is truly made
complete in him. This is how we know we are in him:*
—1 John 2:5

*Dear friends, since God so loved us, we also ought to
love one another.*
—1 John 4:11

A Mother's Prayer Journal

Have you ever wondered whether there is more spiritual life than you are currently experiencing? For most, the answer is usually, "Yes." It is perfectly fine and, I think, natural to expect something deeper, richer and more profound from your spiritual life and a more complete experience of prayer is the key to realizing it. Use these pages to keep a journal about your new life of prayer. Write down who or what you are praying for and use it as both a reminder and a way to stay on a prayerful track.

_____

_____

_____

_____

_____

_____

_____

_____

_____

_____

_____

"Prayer should be the key of the day and the lock of the night."

George Herbert

_____

_____

_____

_____

_____

_____

_____

_____

_____

_____

_____

"Just pray for a tough hide and a tender heart."

Ruth Graham

_____

_____

_____

_____

_____

_____

_____

_____

_____

_____

_____

"All that I am or hope to be I owe to my angel mother. I remember my mother's prayers and they have always followed me. They have clung to me all my life."

Abraham Lincoln

"Sometimes the most important thing in a whole day is the rest we take between two deep breaths, or the turning inwards in prayer for five short minutes."

Etty Hillesum

About the Author

John Bright-Fey teaches classes on prayer, contemplation, and leading a prayerful life. He is the author of several books in the Morning Cup and Whole Heart series. He lives in Birmingham, Alabama.

You may also enjoy these other devotionals in the Morning Cup series. Each one would be a welcomed and treasured gift for the special people in your life.

A Morning Cup of® Prayer for Teachers

ISBN-13: 978-1-57587-265-0
ISBN-10: 1-57587-265-X

A Morning Cup of® Prayer for Friends

ISBN-13: 978-1-57587-263-6
ISBN-10: 1-57587-263-3

A Morning Cup of® Prayer for Women

ISBN-13: 978-1-57587-266-7
ISBN-10: 1-57587-266-8

Prayer at a Glance

Prayer is talking with God

- Anytime
- Anywhere
- Under any circumstance
- About anything
- Authentically

 Step One: Set the stage with solitude, silence, and stillness.

 Step Two: Embrace a prayerful attitude.

 Step Three: Choose your method of prayer.

 Step Four: Talk with God.

 Step Five: Listen to God.

Tear this page out and post it in a handy spot for quick reference to help you make time to pray.